FOCUS ON

FISH

STEVE PARKER

GLOUCESTER PRESS
London · New York · Sydney

Designed and produced by
Aladdin Books Ltd
28 Percy Street
London W1P 9FF

First published in
Great Britain in 1994 by
Watts Books
96 Leonard Street
London EC2A 4RH

ISBN 0 7496 1561 3

Printed in Belgium

Design	David West Children's Book Design
Designer	Flick Killerby
Editor	Jen Green
Picture research	Brooks Krikler Research
Illustrators	David Burroughs

*The author, Steve Parker, is a writer and editor
in the life sciences, health and medicine, who
has written many books for children on science
and nature.*

*The consultant, Oliver Crimmen, is Curator of
Fishes at the Natural History Museum in
London.*

INTRODUCTION

To many people, fishes are small, colourful swimmers in the home aquarium, dark shapes moving in a lake, or a slab of white flesh on a plate. This book opens up the amazing world of fishes to reveal their strange shapes, brilliant colours, speed and agility. It describes how fishes hunt and hide, court and breed, and live out their lives in every watery habitat on our planet, from icy polar seas to tropical swamps, and from a small puddle to the deepest ocean. The book also traces the links between fishes and people through the ages, with information related to geography, literature, history, maths, science, technology and art. The key below shows how these subjects are divided up.

Geography
The symbol of the planet Earth indicates where geographical facts are included in the book. These sections contain descriptions of traditional methods of catching fish around the world.

Language and literature
An open book is the sign for activities and information about language and literature. These sections include a look at the many stories that have been inspired by the world of fish, including the legend of the great white shark.

Science and technology

The microscope symbol indicates information about science and technology. These sections provide many insights into the habits of fish, and describe how certain species have been bred for their beauty.

History

The sign of the scroll and hourglass indicates historical information. These sections explore how fish have been valued and cultivated through the ages. Certain fish products such as caviare, which were once common, are now rare.

Maths

Activities and information related to mathematics are indicated by the symbol of the ruler, protractor and compass. Activities include measuring and comparing your sprint speed with that of the fastest fish.

Art, craft and music

The symbol showing a sheet of music and art tools signals where activities and information about art, crafts and music appear in the book. One project examines how fishes swim and describes how you can make a working model of a moving fish.

CONTENTS

WHAT ARE FISHES?

Fishes are a large and varied group of creatures, all superbly adapted for life under water. They have an inner skeleton based on a backbone, which means they are included in the group of *vertebrate* animals. Their skin is covered with hard scales for protection. They are cold-blooded, and "breathe" (absorb oxygen) under the water by means of gills. Their bodies are streamlined for speed in the water, and they swim by moving their tail and fins. But among the many thousands of fish species, there are exceptions to almost all of these features.

Fish ancestry

Fishes have been swimming around our planet for almost 500 million years. They far outlived the dinosaurs and many other prehistoric animals. Over 350 million years ago, certain fishes evolved limbs and became amphibians, starting four-legged life on land. Today there are over 23,000 species of fishes, more than all the other vertebrates – amphibians, reptiles, birds and mammals – added together. The basic fish design has changed remarkably little through the immense time of prehistory. But there are many variations in shape and size.

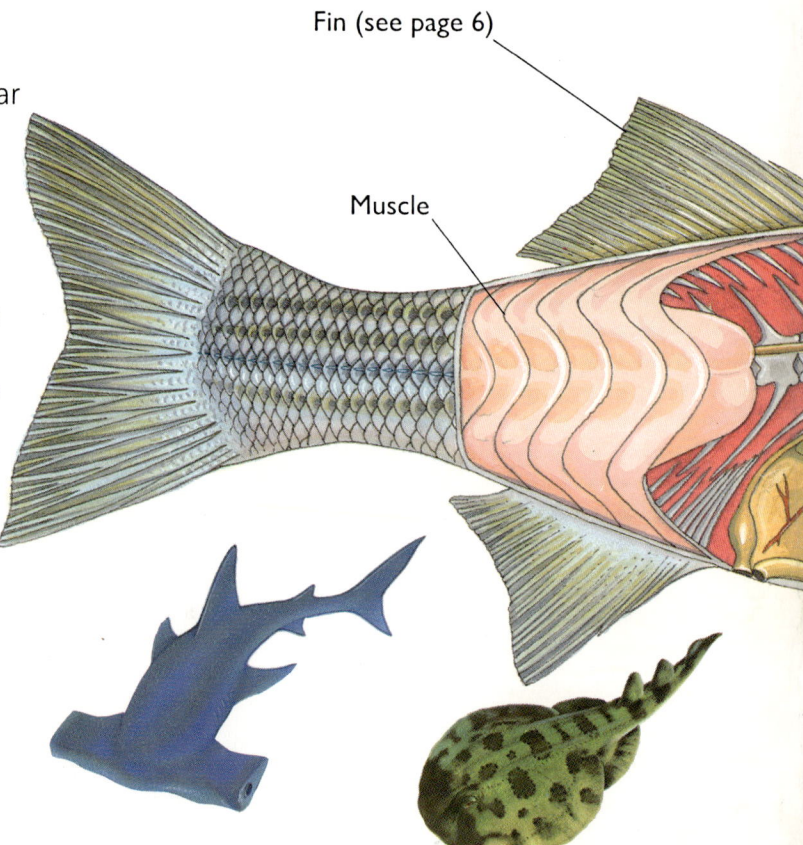

Fin (see page 6)

Muscle

Moorish idol

Sunfish

Hammerhead shark

Electric ray

Fossil fishes
Some rocks contain the bones of fish, turned to stone and preserved as fossils. The Old Red Sandstones from Scotland, formed 408-360 million years ago, have yielded thousands of fossil specimens.

Small world
Some fishes are free to roam the oceans, but others live in the tiniest areas. The most restricted is the Devil's Hole pupfish, *Cyprinodon diabolis*. These silvery little fishes live in just one pool, in the desert floor of Nevada, in the United States. Their entire world is a body of water hardly larger than a school classroom.

Various creatures are called "fish", for no better reason than that they live in water. But they are not true fish. They include jellyfish (which are in fact members of the group of animals known as cnidarians), starfish (which are echinoderms), shellfish (a name given to molluscs) and crayfish (crustaceans). Some water-dwellers also look and live like fish, but again, they are not. They include whales and dolphins,

Blue whale

which are warm-blooded, air-breathing mammals, like you. Seals and sea lions are also mammals, although they are at home in the water. Penguins and divers swim as well as fish, but they are birds.

Starfish

Swim bladder for buoyancy

Brain

Gills (see page 7)

Smell organ

Heart

Intestine

Stomach

Kidney

Inside a fish

The skeleton of a fish is made from bone in most species, but from cartilage (gristle) in sharks, skates and rays. It consists of a skull which houses the small brain, numerous backbones (vertebrae), and ribs. The upper body is mainly blocks of muscle to manipulate the tail for swimming. The lower body contains the internal organs, which are similar to most other vertebrates – the heart and main blood vessels, digestive organs such as the stomach and intestines, and the reproductive parts.

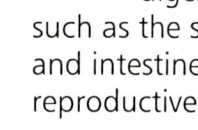

Butterfish

Oarfish

The biggest fish is the whale shark (shown right), which can grow to 15 metres in length and 20 tonnes in weight. The smallest fish is a dwarf goby from the Indian Ocean (below), at just 13 millimetres long. The longest bony fish is the oarfish, which grows up to 12 metres long.

FINS, SCALES & GILLS

Three characteristic features of animal life are movement, respiration (breathing) and body protection. In most fishes, movement is provided by the tail and fins. The tail propels the fish forward, and the other fins are used for steering and manoeuvring. The fish is protected by the scales over its body surface. They are hard and tough, but they also allow flexibility, so the body can bend and twist as the fish moves. Breathing is carried out by the gills, just behind the eyes. Fishes, like other animals, need a continuous supply of oxygen to survive. The gills absorb oxygen which is dissolved in the water.

Fins

A typical fish has between seven and ten fins, although some, like eels, have only three or four. The biggest is the caudal fin – the tail. The median fins on the back and belly, along the mid-line of the fish, give stability. The paired fins on either side are used for steering. Each fin is made from a stretchy substance that is supported by thin rods of cartilage or bone, the fin rays. Muscles at the base of the fin move and tilt the fin rays, to alter the shape of the fin.

Sprint champion
The fastest fish is the sailfish, which can sprint-swim at 110 kph (nearly 70 mph). It would take three seconds to cover 100 metres. Measure your own sprint speed by timing yourself in a run of 100 metres. How do you compare to the sailfish?

First dorsal fin

Caudal fin (tail)

Second dorsal fin

Anal fin

Pelvic fin

Pectoral fin

Sandpaper skin
Sharks have special types of scales called denticles (close-up shown right). They are like tiny pointed teeth embedded in the skin. The denticles make sharkskin "leather" very tough and rough. Sharkskin has been used to make waistcoats, belts, boots and other articles of clothing, and also as an abrasive, like sandpaper.

Scales
Most fish are covered almost completely with scales. Each scale has a similar shape to your fingernail, and is made of a bony substance. The base or root of the scale is embedded in the skin, but the rest is not attached. The scales lie against the body and overlap like tiles on a roof. They are covered with slimy mucus to protect the fish and allow it to glide through the water.

Water flow
Water flows in through the mouth, over the gills where the oxygen is absorbed, and out behind the gill cover.

Gill filaments
These are small, thin flaps that absorb the maximum oxygen.

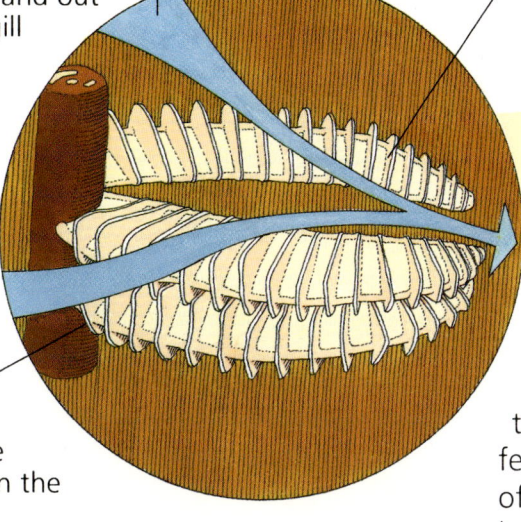

Gill arch
The gill filaments are supported on the gill arch.

Oxygen flow
Oxygen from the water passes through the very thin surfaces of the gill filaments into the bloodstream, and is then distributed around the body.

Gills
The gills of a fish do the same job as the lungs of a land animal – they take in the oxygen essential for life, and absorb it into the bloodstream. The gills are delicate, feather-shaped parts that have a rich supply of blood inside. They are dark red in colour because they are filled with blood. There are usually four or five sets of gills on either side of the head, covered and protected by a flap known as the gill cover or operculum. Sharks do not have an operculum (see page 16).

A "living fossil"
Fossils show that the group of fishes called coelacanths were common between 350 and 70 million years ago. But then they died out – or at least, so scientists believed. Then a living coelacanth was caught in 1938 off south-east Africa. More have been observed and caught off the nearby Comoro Islands. The coelacanth has fleshy-based or lobed fins. It is related to the first fish that crawled onto land over 350 million years ago, to become amphibians.

Gasping for breath
At warm temperatures water contains less oxygen than at cool temperatures. So hot conditions mean that less oxygen is available for a fish to absorb. This is made worse if a pool containing fish starts to dry out, crowding them into a smaller volume of water. The fish may come to the surface and "gasp for air". Lungfish are specialised to take in oxygen from the air (see page 19).

COLOUR, SHAPE, MOVEMENT

Like the mackerel shown left, many fish are streamlined in shape, to move swiftly and smoothly through the water. Most are silvery or greeny-blue in colour, to blend in with the water around them. However, there are many variations on this basic design. Some fish are shaped and coloured to resemble the wafting seaweed or seabed rocks of their surroundings, for camouflage. Others have bright colours and patterns, to advertise the fact that they are poisonous or have horrible-tasting flesh. Would-be predators recognise these colours and keep away.

The slinky swimmer

You can make a model of a flexible fish using card and split-pins. Cut out the fish's body in five segments, as shown below. Cut flaps at the top and bottom of each segment, and make holes in the flaps for the split-pins. Join the segments by pushing the pins through the holes. These joints represent the joints between the vertebrae, or separate backbones. Now hold your fish by the tail and twist it from side to side. See how its body wriggles into S-shape curves, as though swimming.

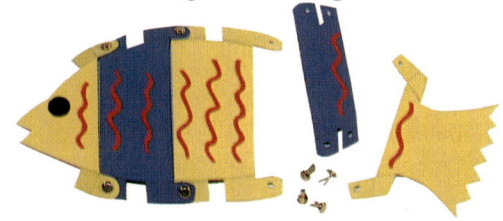

The plaice can alter its colour to blend in with the sea bed.

Shapes and patterns

Biologists study a fish's shape and colour in relation to its natural surroundings. A brightly coloured fish swimming in a bare aquarium looks very conspicuous. But in its natural habitat of the coral reef, the fish's bright colours blend in with the equally bright hues of corals, rocks and weeds, and it becomes almost unnoticed. The John Dory (shown right) looks large and ungainly from the side. But from the front, it is extremely thin. This presents a very small area for other fish to see, which may help it to approach its prey head-on in the dim waters, without being noticed.

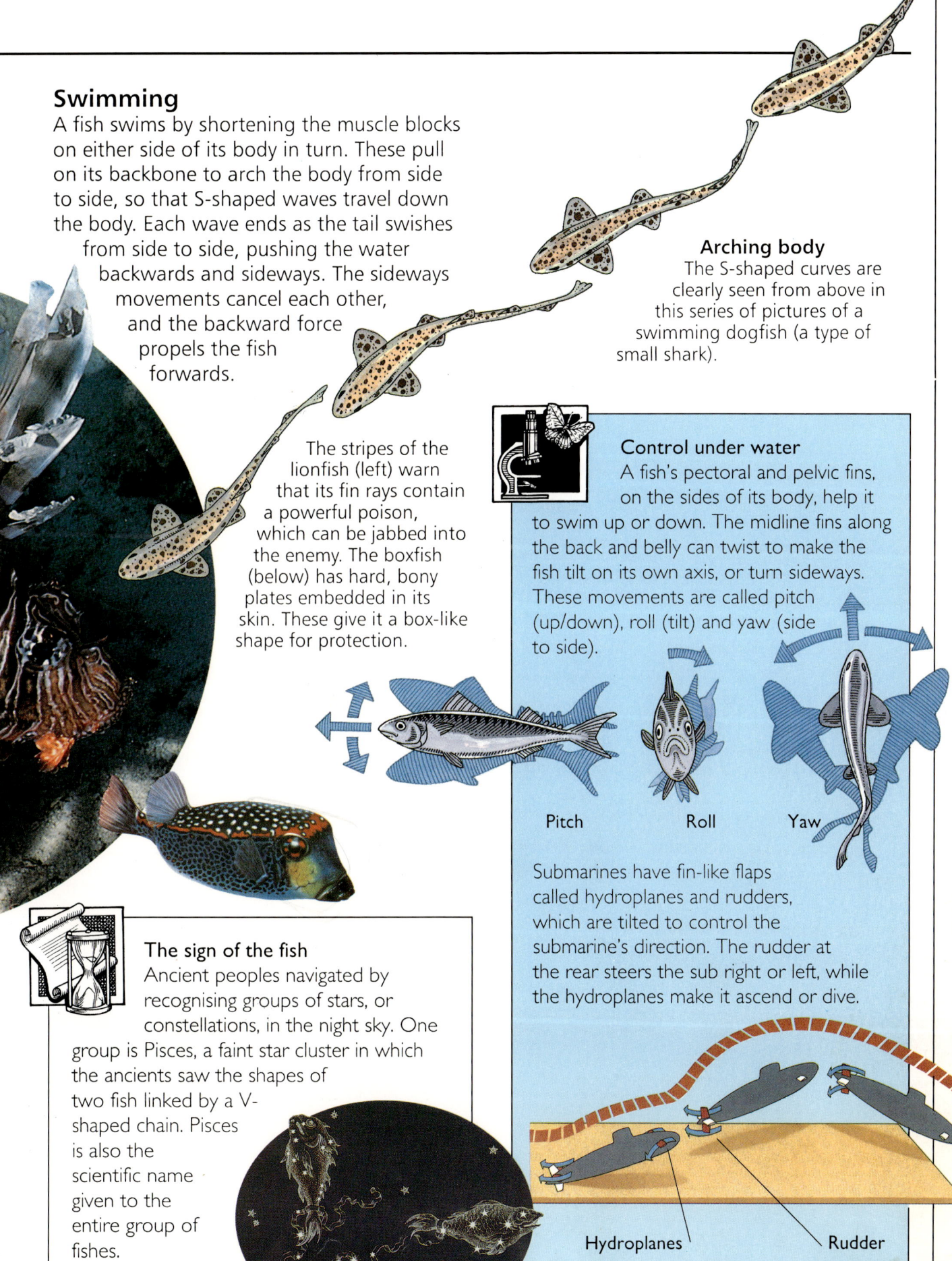

Swimming

A fish swims by shortening the muscle blocks on either side of its body in turn. These pull on its backbone to arch the body from side to side, so that S-shaped waves travel down the body. Each wave ends as the tail swishes from side to side, pushing the water backwards and sideways. The sideways movements cancel each other, and the backward force propels the fish forwards.

The stripes of the lionfish (left) warn that its fin rays contain a powerful poison, which can be jabbed into the enemy. The boxfish (below) has hard, bony plates embedded in its skin. These give it a box-like shape for protection.

Arching body

The S-shaped curves are clearly seen from above in this series of pictures of a swimming dogfish (a type of small shark).

Control under water

A fish's pectoral and pelvic fins, on the sides of its body, help it to swim up or down. The midline fins along the back and belly can twist to make the fish tilt on its own axis, or turn sideways. These movements are called pitch (up/down), roll (tilt) and yaw (side to side).

Pitch   Roll   Yaw

Submarines have fin-like flaps called hydroplanes and rudders, which are tilted to control the submarine's direction. The rudder at the rear steers the sub right or left, while the hydroplanes make it ascend or dive.

Hydroplanes   Rudder

The sign of the fish

Ancient peoples navigated by recognising groups of stars, or constellations, in the night sky. One group is Pisces, a faint star cluster in which the ancients saw the shapes of two fish linked by a V-shaped chain. Pisces is also the scientific name given to the entire group of fishes.

FEEDING & DEFENCE

To survive, a fish must eat and avoid being eaten. Most fish have strong jaws and many teeth for feeding. Some of the teeth are found along the edges of the jaws. Others, known as pharyngeal teeth, are found inside the back of the mouth, where they crush and squash the food as the fish "chews". To avoid being eaten, fish have developed an astonishing array of self-defence methods. Some use their great speed to flee from their enemies. Others have poisonous spines or flesh, or use special survival tactics to make themselves unpalatable to predators.

Fish in the food chain
The feeding links between different animals build up into food chains showing who eats whom. Land animals can join the chains if they enter the water, and fish can enter land-based food chains when caught. William Shakespeare showed how a food chain can come full circle when he wrote in *Hamlet:* "A man may fish with the worm that hath eat of a king, and eat of the fish that hath fed of that worm." This could be shown as: Man (king) > eaten by worm > eaten by fish > eaten by man > and so on. Can you draw a diagram of this?

Water arrows
The archerfish from tropical areas can shoot down prey such as insects above the surface with an "arrow" of water. This hits the prey, knocking it into the water, and the archerfish snaps it up.

Scrape and rasp
The parrotfish is named for its hard, horny mouth, shaped like the beak of a bird. The mouth is formed from fused-together teeth and is ideal for scraping and rubbing plants and corals from rocks.

Stealthy ambush
The pike has a vast mouth armed with pointed teeth. It lurks among the weeds until an unwary victim is close. The pike surges forward and closes its large jaws over the meal.

Picky eater
The forceps fish has a long, thin snout with a tiny mouth at the end. It can poke this into crevices in the coral reef, and even into the stony cups of the corals themselves, to grab the small, anemone-like coral animals (polyps).

Mouths and food

Most fish specialise in a certain type of food. Their mouthparts are adapted to deal with their particular diet. Fish with little, weak mouths consume soft, small items such as worms in the mud. Some hunting fish have bigger mouths with strong, blade-like teeth that can tear chunks from large prey. Predatory fish that catch slippery, struggling victims and swallow them whole have huge mouths with thin, needle-shaped, backward-pointing fangs. Hard, horny, beak-like mouths are designed to rub and rasp plant food.

Enemies of fish

Fish fall prey to bigger fish and other animals that live in and out of water. They are hunted by predators from above, such as gulls, pelicans, fishing-bats and fish-eagles (pictured here). Fish-eaters on the bank, such as bears, hook them out with long, clawed paws. Animals such as otters and seals that were originally based on land have evolved to swim as fast as the fish they catch.

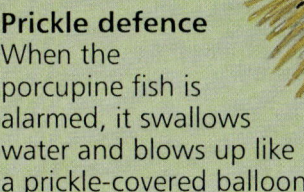

Poison defence
The back spines of the stonefish contain a powerful venom (poison). It can raise the spines, so they jab into enemies.

Prickle defence
When the porcupine fish is alarmed, it swallows water and blows up like a prickle-covered balloon.

Throw in another slave

In Ancient Rome, rich people kept various strange beasts as pets. Some had large tanks for moray eels – muscular eels up to two metres long, with many sharp teeth. The sea water had to be changed regularly and was often carried dozens of kilometres by teams of servants. Prize eels were much treasured, awarded gifts, and even supposedly given disobedient slaves to eat, as a warning to other slaves.

Harvest from the sea
Fish are an important source of food for many peoples, especially for island nations who lack the land area for farming. Fish provide their main source of protein for a balanced diet. Sushi (shown right) is a dish of sliced raw fish. However, parts of some fish are poisonous. The traditional Japanese delicacy fugu is made from the liver and other parts of the pufferfish, which are poisonous when raw. If not cooked properly, the poison remains in the food and can kill the eater.

SENSES

When we swim in the underwater world, we have to make the best of our human senses, which are designed for working in air. Sounds are muffled and strange, and we are rocked to and fro by unfamiliar water movements. Fish have senses that are adapted to gather amazing amounts of information from their surroundings. Pressure detectors along the sides of their bodies are sensitive to swirls and currents of water. They warn the fish that there are objects nearby obstructing the water flow, or that other aquatic creatures are moving about.

Sight

The surface waters of a sheltered lake or calm sea are bright and clear. Fish such as the tropical triggerfish (shown above) are able to use their eyes, which are structurally quite similar to our own. But 200 metres below the surface in any body of water, all the sunlight begins to be filtered out, and it becomes pitch black. Most deep-water fish have small eyes, or none at all. Mid-water fish such as the lanternfish (shown right) have extremely large eyes, to gather as much of the dim light as possible.

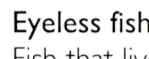

Eyeless fish

Fish that live in the endless darkness of caves have little use for eyes. So over millions of years of evolution, their eyes have become small or disappeared altogether. The Ozark cavefish from North America is one of many blind fish from caverns around the world. But it has a well-developed lateral line system, for monitoring water currents.

Four-eyed fish

Light refracts (bends and slows down) as it goes into water. This means the lens of the eye needs to be more powerful in water compared to air. A fish out of water sees a blurred view – except the four-eyed fish from Central and South America. It has two eyes, but each has two parts. The lower half has the usual underwater lens. The upper half's lens is weaker, for seeing in air.

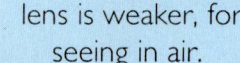

Dusky perch

Lateral line

Feeling

A fish's skin can sense being touched. A fish also has a sensory part called the lateral line, a thin strip along each side of its body. This enables the fish to detect ripples and currents in the water. Water movements give valuable information about possible predators or prey nearby. It is also important in fish who gather together into a shoal, for feeding and safety. As each fish moves, its neighbours can sense changes of speed and direction using their lateral lines, and move in the same way.

Feeding frenzy

The piranha has a mouthful of sharp teeth like triangular blades. If a shoal senses blood from a wounded creature in the water, the fish go into an uncontrolled "feeding frenzy", slashing and tearing at the victim. In Ian Fleming's *James Bond* books piranhas were used by the villains to dispose of their enemies.

The catfish has tiny chemosensors for tasting in and around its mouth, on its long whiskery barbels, and over most of its body, too.

Smell and taste

For land animals such as humans, smell and taste are separate senses. Smells come through the air. But in water they are less distinct, since both scents and flavours spread through the water. For this reason smell and taste are merged together and called the chemosenses, since they detect various chemicals floating in the water. Most fish have nostrils which open into a chamber called the olfactory cavity, for long-distance "smells", and taste buds in and around their mouths, for nearby "tastes".

Sensing with electricity

Certain fish can make and sense electricity. The elephant-snout fish makes weak pulses of electricity using specialised body muscles. These pass through water and are detected by electrosensors on its head. Any objects in the way distort the electric field, and the fish finds its way and its food by this electrical sense. Electric eels and electric rays (below) have blocks of specialised body muscles that produce powerful bursts of electricity, up to 500 volts, to stun enemies and victims.

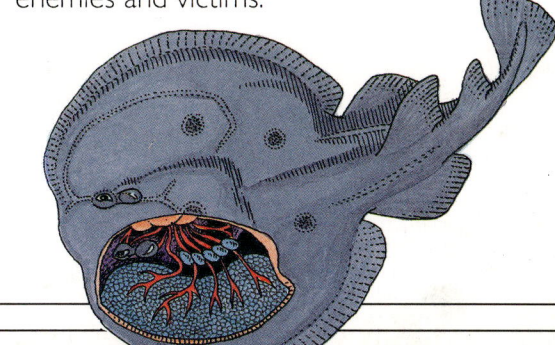

COURTSHIP & BREEDING

Animals use courtship behaviour to make sure that they are pairing up with a mate of the same species, and one who is fit and healthy. In this way, the mating is likely to produce healthy offspring. Fish courtship is not usually so spectacular as it is in many birds and mammals. Most fish come together only fleetingly to mate, and then go their own way again. However, some pond and coral reef fish use visual displays and courtship behaviour in the brightly-lit waters of their habitats.

Courting and caring

In most species of fish, the female lays her eggs (roe), the male adds his milky sperm (milt) to fertilise them, and then the eggs are left on their own. However, some fish have complex courtships, and care for their babies. The male stickleback (below) entices a female to his nest by showing off his bright breeding colours. He also cares for his young as they develop in the nest. So does the male seahorse, in a "pocket" on his belly.

Father gives birth

The seahorse is a strangely-shaped fish related to the stickleback. After the female lays her eggs, the male gathers them into the brood pouch on his front. The babies develop in this protected place. A few weeks later their father "gives birth" through the small opening of the pouch.

The mating dance

In spring, the male stickleback's underside goes bright red and his eyes turn bright blue. He builds a nest of plant debris on the bottom. Then he swims around a female in a zig-zag courting dance, attracting her with his bright colours. He encourages her to the nest. She lays her eggs and he adds his sperm – the process known as spawning.

Prized eggs

Sturgeons are massive fish three to four metres long, with large back scales and pointed snouts. The salted, unlaid eggs of the female sturgeon form the delicacy called caviare. At one time sturgeons were common, and even poor people ate caviare. But centuries of overfishing have made sturgeons very rare, and caviare very expensive.

Bred for beauty

For centuries, people have selected and bred together certain specimens of fish. This has been done to enhance their natural shapes and colours, or in the hope of producing new features such as frilly fins or goggle eyes. Koi and other carp have been bred in China and Japan for over 4,000 years. The goldfish was produced by selective breeding about 1,600 years ago.

Places for protection

Some fish lay their eggs in a protected place, such as under a rock or among weeds, where they are less likely to be noticed and eaten by other fish. Many cichlids, freshwater fish from warm climates, keep their eggs in their mouths! Usually the female does this, a process known as mouth-brooding. Other fish, like sharks and rays, lay eggs with tough, leathery cases (below) that protect the developing young inside.

Baby cichlids swim in a cloud around the mother's head. But they are ready to dash back into her mouth if danger threatens.

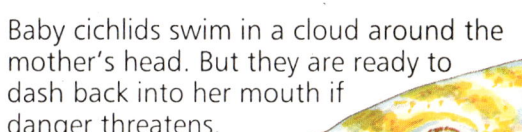

Life cycle of the salmon

Salmon spawn (lay eggs and sperm) in the shallow waters of small inland streams. The eggs hatch and the young salmon spend several years in the river, before migrating to sea where they become mature. To breed, the adults battle from the sea and make their way upriver. Surveys on tagged fish show that each salmon returns to the very stream where it hatched. It probably finds its way by its chemosenses (see page 13).

Hanger-on

In the vast, inky depths of the sea, it is difficult to find a suitable partner. So when a male deep-sea anglerfish meets a female, he joins himself to her body. He becomes more and more firmly attached until his body is fused to hers. The female has a male at hand ready to fertilise her eggs. But she also has one or several hangers-on or "parasites" who she carries everywhere, and who she has to supply with food.

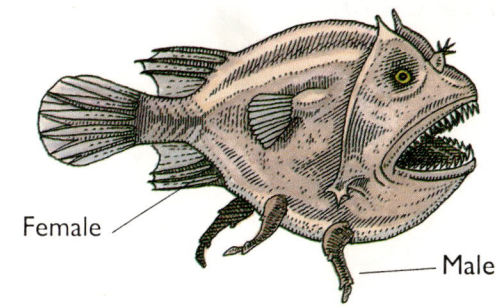

Female

Male

SHARKS & THEIR COUSINS

Sharks were some of the first fish to appear on Earth. They have cruised the seas, almost unchanged, for more than 300 million years. The shark skeleton is made not of bone, as in most other fish, but of the tough, bendy substance called cartilage (gristle). Rays and skates also have cartilaginous skeletons. So do the deep-sea fish known as chimaeras or ratfish, which have large heads and eyes, and thin tapering tails. All these fish are in their own major group, the Chondrichthyes or cartilaginous fish, with about 725 species.

The shape of the killer

All sharks are supreme predators. Many, like the mako and tiger shark, are sleek and streamlined for fast pursuit and charging at a victim. Others, like the wobbegong or carpet shark (below) are less active, relying on their camouflage and a sudden lunge when the victim comes close. Their bodies are flattened, and they lie on the sea bed, disguised as weed-covered rocks.

Hammer head

The hammerhead shark has its eyes and nostrils on wide stalks. This shape may help to sense the direction of prey in the water.

Hero of the deep

A hungry shark will attack almost anything, including a boat's hull! The speed and power of man-eaters such as the great white and the hammerhead have long been feared. A great white shark starred in the book *Jaws* by Peter Benchley. A series of films was based on this book, using film of real sharks and jointed models.

JAWS

Sensitive hunter

The shark is bristling with senses designed to locate prey, alive or dead. It detects blood or body fluids in the water from several kilometres away. As it closes in, its lateral line system picks up water currents created by the prey's movements. Electrical sensors on its head detect tiny currents of electricity generated by the prey's active muscles. At close range, the shark uses its eyesight for the final fierce charge.

Sharks do not have gill covers (see page 7). Instead each gill has a separate slit.

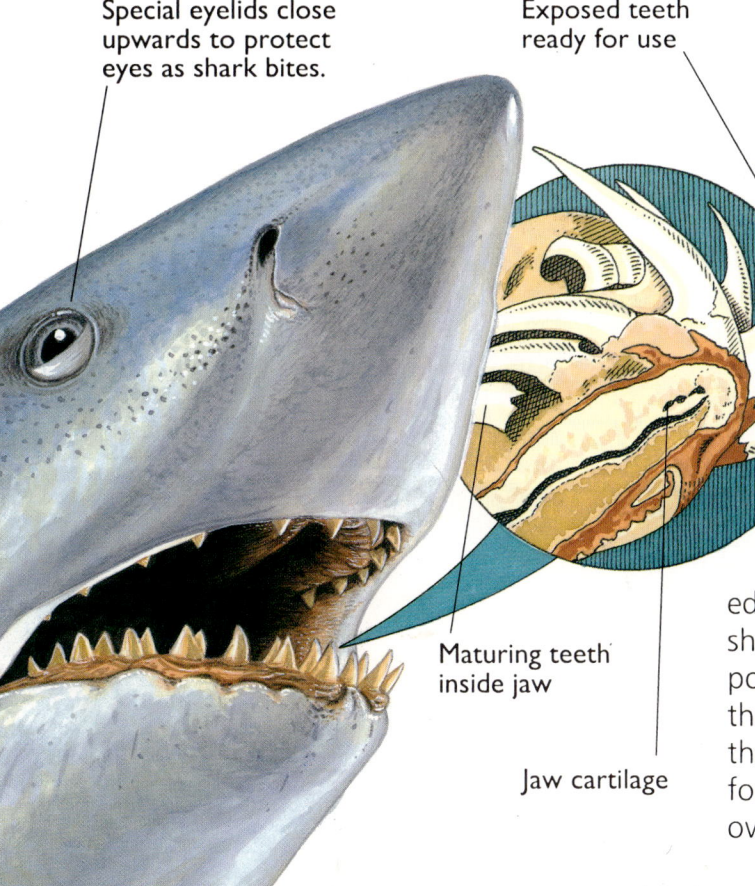

Ray-eating ray
The common skate is a large, heavy ray up to two metres wide. It is a fierce predator of fish, including other rays.

Skates and rays

These cartilaginous fish have evolved for a mainly bottom-dwelling lifestyle. The sides of their bodies have become wide and flattened into "wings". These are flapped up and down for swimming. Most skates and rays feed on the sea bed, scavenging on bits of dead and dying animals, and grubbing up shellfish, worms and other creatures from the sand and mud. They also rest hidden on the bottom, covering themselves with sand or with weeds.

Blond ray
The dark spots of this ray provide excellent camouflage on the mottled sea bed. It grows about one metre long.

Special eyelids close upwards to protect eyes as shark bites.

Exposed teeth ready for use

Maturing teeth inside jaw

Jaw cartilage

New teeth for old

A shark never stops growing new teeth. They form in rows on the insides of the jaws, then move around to the edges, where they are ready for use. As the shark bites and tears a victim, some of its pointed, razor-sharp teeth break off, since they are only anchored in the skin and not in the jaw itself. However, new teeth soon move forward to take their place. Some sharks have over 3,000 teeth in their mouths.

A FISH OUT OF WATER

Most fish cannot live out of water for more than a few minutes – about as long as you could survive under it. Hooked from the sea or river, most fish will soon die of suffocation. But several types of fish can live in air for many hours. Some inhabit shallow pools in tropical places, where the warm water is very low in dissolved oxygen, and gills can only obtain limited amounts for breathing. Others dwell in places where the pools often dry out. They must either go into a deep sleep, called torpor, below the muddy surface, and wait for the rains to refill the pool, or set off across land to look for a new home.

A reverse aqualung
The aqualung contains compressed air. Divers breathe the air through a special pressure-reducing valve, so that they can stay underwater for long periods. The mudskipper (below) does the reverse. It brings gill-fulls of water up into the air, and breathes the oxygen in the water.

Moving on land
The eel is a very hardy fish. It can survive in water that is too polluted for many other fish, and it can eat almost any kind of food. It is very slippery and writhes so strongly that it is difficult for predators to grip and catch. If a river or lake becomes too polluted or dries out, the eel can even wriggle over land to find a new patch of water. It keeps to damp vegetation, moving like a snake with S-shaped curves of its body. The slimy mucus covering its body prevents it from drying out, and allows it to slide through dense vegetation or between rocks and stones. Mature eels migrate to the sea for breeding (see page 27), and they may also travel over land at this time.

Walking and breathing
Mudskippers live in the muddy mangrove swamps along tropical coasts and estuaries. They can walk and even skitter fast on their strong, arm-like pectoral fins. They breathe by filling their large gill chambers with water. They regularly take a dip in a tidal pool to change the water in their gill chambers and so get fresh oxygen supplies. Mudskippers can live for a time in fresh water, as well as the normal sea water.

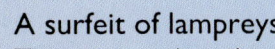

A surfeit of lampreys

The very ancient, jawless, eel-shaped fish called lampreys can survive out of water for a time. These are parasites, drinking the blood from larger fish through their sucker-like mouths. Lampreys were once common in Britain, and eaten in large quantities by people. However the slippery mucus over their bodies is poisonous, and must be scraped off before eating. In 1135 King Henry I of England died, supposedly poisoned by having eaten too many lampreys.

Asleep in the mud

Three main types of lungfish live in the fresh waters of Amazonian South America, central and southern Africa, and north-eastern Australia. If its waters dry up, the African lungfish (above) wriggles into the mud and produces a slimy bag around itself. This hardens into a cocoon case, and the fish can survive in this condition for two or three years.

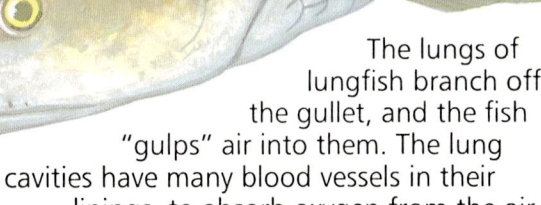

Blood vessels

Gas space

The lungs of lungfish branch off the gullet, and the fish "gulps" air into them. The lung cavities have many blood vessels in their linings, to absorb oxygen from the air.

The bare bones

The Aboriginal people of Australia have been producing rock art for over 30,000 years. Many of the pictures feature animals, and some of them are "X-ray images" showing the bones and organs inside the creature. Fish, including the Australian lungfish, figure in the paintings, which show the pattern of the skull, backbone and ribs.

It's raining fish

There have been many instances reported of rainstorms showering down not only water, but also fish. Among the species which have poured down from the clouds are trout and sticklebacks. It is thought that such an event occurs when powerful swirling winds, as in a tornado, pass over a body of water and suck up the water – and the fish – as a waterspout. The fish are swept into the cloud and then fall with the rain.

FISH OF LAKES & RIVERS

The fresh waters of the world make up only about three per cent of all the water on Earth. Yet they represent a great variety of habitats, from small ponds to deep lakes, fast-flowing brooks to sluggish rivers, still canals and ditches, foaming waterfalls, and dark underground pools and streams. Fish have adapted to all of these different habitats. Some require particular conditions such as a special diet, or water with a certain amount of oxygen. Other fish, such as sticklebacks and loaches, are tough and hardy, and can survive almost anywhere.

Freshwater giant
The arapaima (pirarucu) is one of the largest freshwater fish. It lives in the rivers, lakes and flooded forests of the Amazon region in South America. These monsters may have once grown up to five metres long.

Coolie loach

Alewife

Small-mouthed bass

Arapaima

Knifefish

Eye spy
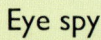
The ripples and reflections on the water's surface make it difficult to see the fish below. You can make a "window" on their watery world using a plastic bucket. Cut out the bottom of the bucket with a knife (you may need an adult to help with this). Cover the hole with strong clingfilm or a sheet of clear plastic. Tape the edges of this in place around the lower sides of the bucket, to make a waterproof seal. Hold the bucket's bottom just below the water's surface, and you should have a clear view into the aquatic environment.

Introductions

People have taken certain species of fish from their natural homes and "introduced" them to new areas. The gambusia (1) from America has been introduced to many parts of the world because it eats mosquito larvae, and so helps to control the disease malaria. The rainbow trout (2) was introduced to Europe from North America, for angling and food. But these newcomers can cause problems. The large Nile perch (3) has been introduced to other African rivers and lakes, as a food source. But it eats many smaller fish and upsets the local balance of nature.

Living conditions

To us, one pond may look much like another. But conditions in the water are often very different. One major condition is water temperature. Warmer water holds less oxygen (see page 7). But some fish of tropical freshwater, like the arapaima, can gulp oxygen directly from the air. Still water holds less oxygen than running water, but a fast flow means that fishes such as trout and grayling must battle against the current or hide under rocks, to prevent being swept away. Each fish species can tolerate a certain range in these living conditions.

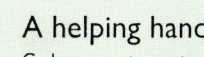

A helping hand

Salmon, trout, eels and other freshwater fish travel on long migrations to and from the sea, essential to their breeding cycle. If a dam or barrage is built across a river, it can form an impassable barrier. A stepped series of pools, called a fish ladder, may be constructed to one side so that the fish can leap and wriggle up or down. Some dams have tunnels with meshes designed to retain fish. The fish are collected and transported to safety.

Neon tetra

Bluegill sunfish

Shag

Rainbow darter

2

3

1

Stew ponds

In medieval times, fish flesh was a valuable addition to the weekly diet. Medieval monks kept carp and other fish in protected, isolated pools known as stew ponds. These ponds are mentioned in the Domesday Book survey of Norman England, carried out for William I (the Conqueror) in 1085-86.

FISH OF SHORES & REEFS

The shallow waters along the seashore provide a wide range of fish habitats, from tidal mudflats to sandbanks and rocky coasts. In tropical areas, coral reefs can support a great variety of life. Nutrients are plentiful, and the bright sun provides lots of light, so many seaweeds and other plants can grow. These plants are the basic food for all the forms of animal life, including myriad worms, crabs, starfish and shellfish, which thrive in the warm, shallow waters. They, in turn, provide food for a dazzling array of fish. In contrast, the shoreline of a wide beach is much emptier of fish.

Nooks and crannies
The blenny and rock goby use rocks and boulders to shelter from predators and ambush prey. The clingfish can stick to overhanging rocks with its sucker-like fins.

Clingfish

Lumpsucker

Rock goby

Grunion

Butterfish

Blenny

Tropical paradise
Many people dream of "getting away from it all" on a deserted tropical island. In 1719 the English writer Daniel Defoe based his adventure story *Robinson Crusoe* on the experiences of a real sailor named Alexander Selkirk. The book tells of a lonely castaway struggling to survive on a small island, beset by lack of food, water and shelter, and plagued by insect pests, pirates and islanders. Not such a paradise?

Traditional fishing
Around the world's coastlines, people use various traditional fishing methods to catch what they need from the sea. The Inuit people of northern North America fish from the shore or along coastal rivers, using nets, and spears, harpoons and hooks carved from natural materials such as walrus tusks or whalebone. However, these traditional ways of life are becoming ever more difficult to preserve.

The perils of the tide

Shores and reefs can be treacherous places for fish, because of the tides. As the tide falls, it can leave fish marooned in pools. The butterfish is named from its tough, slippery, slimy skin. This enables it to wriggle from under rolling pebbles, and prevents it from drying out as it flaps over the rocks from one pool to another. Shore fish such as gobies and blennies can withstand great variations in temperature and salinity (salt concentration), as well as buffeting by waves and rolling boulders.

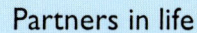

Partners in life

Certain fish team up with quite different animals, in relationships beneficial to both. Clownfish swim among the stinging tentacles of anemones. Their bodies are covered in mucus that provides a barrier to the stings. The clownfish are safe from attack while the anemone consumes the food they drop. This partnership is called symbiosis.

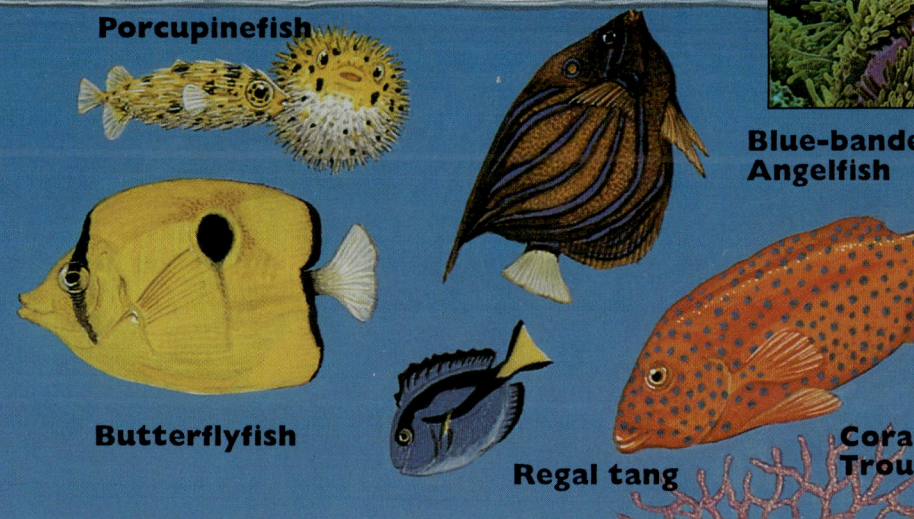

Porcupinefish

Blue-banded Angelfish

Clownfish

Butterflyfish

Regal tang

Coral Trout

Warm and shallow

Coral reefs are rich environments for fish and other sea life, but they form only in certain places around the world. The water must be very clean, and warm – preferably between 22 and 26°C all year – with a salt concentration of between 25 and 40 parts per thousand. The basis of the reef is the coral polyp, a tiny animal like a miniature jellyfish. Polyps grow in their millions and build hard, chalky cup-shaped skeletons around their bodies, for protection. As they die, more polyps grow on top. Over hundreds of years, billions of coral skeletons accumulate, and the rocky reef grows. The corals are food for hundreds of fish.

FISH OF THE OPEN OCEAN

More than two-thirds of the Earth's surface is covered by sea. Fish are the dominant form of life. Their world is fully three-dimensional, unlike that of most land-based creatures, who inhabit the narrow layer just above, on and below dry ground. In the middle of the sea, water stretches for thousands of kilometres on all sides – and for kilometres above and below. There is nowhere to hide. The open ocean is ruled by fast, powerful swimmers, like marlins, swordfish, tunas and sharks.

Sharp-nosed
The swordfish's sharp snout may be designed to slash and stab at smaller fish, for food.

Blue marlin

Swordfish

Herring

Shoal numbers
Herring are one of the most numerous fish in the sea. When danger threatens, they gather together. In a dense, concentrated shoal there may be 20 herring in a cubic metre of seawater. In the past, before overfishing depleted their numbers, some shoals of herring measured one kilometre both long and wide, and extended from the surface to 30 metres deep. Can you work out how many individual herring there would be in one of these gigantic shoals?

Answer: About six million

The myth of the mermaid
For old-time sailors many months at sea, sparse food, monotonous routine and only the flat ocean on all sides combined to play tricks on the mind. In the days of sailing ships, mariners sometimes "saw" mermaids, with the head and torso of a woman, but the tail of a fish. The mermaid legend could have arisen from distant sightings of sea-cows, marine mammals with rounded faces.

Invisible barriers

Although the oceans may look featureless to us, the water is not all the same. Cold currents well up from below, bringing minerals and nutrients. Temperate regions receive warm currents from the tropics, and cooler water from the poles. The surface waters are the most populated, because they are warm and sunlight allows the growth of plankton, tiny floating plants and animals. These are eaten by small animals who are food for fish such as herring and mackerel, which form huge shoals. They in turn are hunted by large predators such as dolphin-fish and tunas.

Flyingfish

Dolphinfish

Yellowfin tuna (tunny)

Gliding to safety

The flyingfish cannot truly fly. But it can build up swimming speed in the water and then leap above the surface, gliding for more than 100 metres at heights of up to two metres. Its "wings" are very large pectoral and/or pelvic fins, depending on the species. The fish glides to escape from fast predators such as marlins and tunas.

Gone fishing

Island peoples around the world who depend on fish as a food source have created many different kinds of fishing vessels. Pacific islanders use outrigger canoes. The canoe hull is made from a hollowed-out tree trunk, and the outrigger gives stability when hauling in large catches or in the surf.

FISH OF SEA BED & DEEP

The terrain of the sea bed is varied, like the surface of the land. There are sandy deserts, cliffs, forests of tall seaweeds or fields of waving seagrass, piles of rocks and deep canyons. Fish rest, hide and hunt here. Below about 500 metres all light has gone, the temperature falls to only a few degrees, and the huge weight of the water above increases the pressure to many tonnes per square centimetre. In terms of volume, this is the biggest and most mysterious habitat on Earth, and home to some of the most extraordinary of all fish.

Fish of the abyss

Depths greater than 2,000 metres (that's over a mile) are termed the abyssal zone. It is normally pitch black, so body colours are useless. Some fish that live there have enormous mouths armed with back-pointing teeth, and stretchy stomachs, since meals are few and far between.

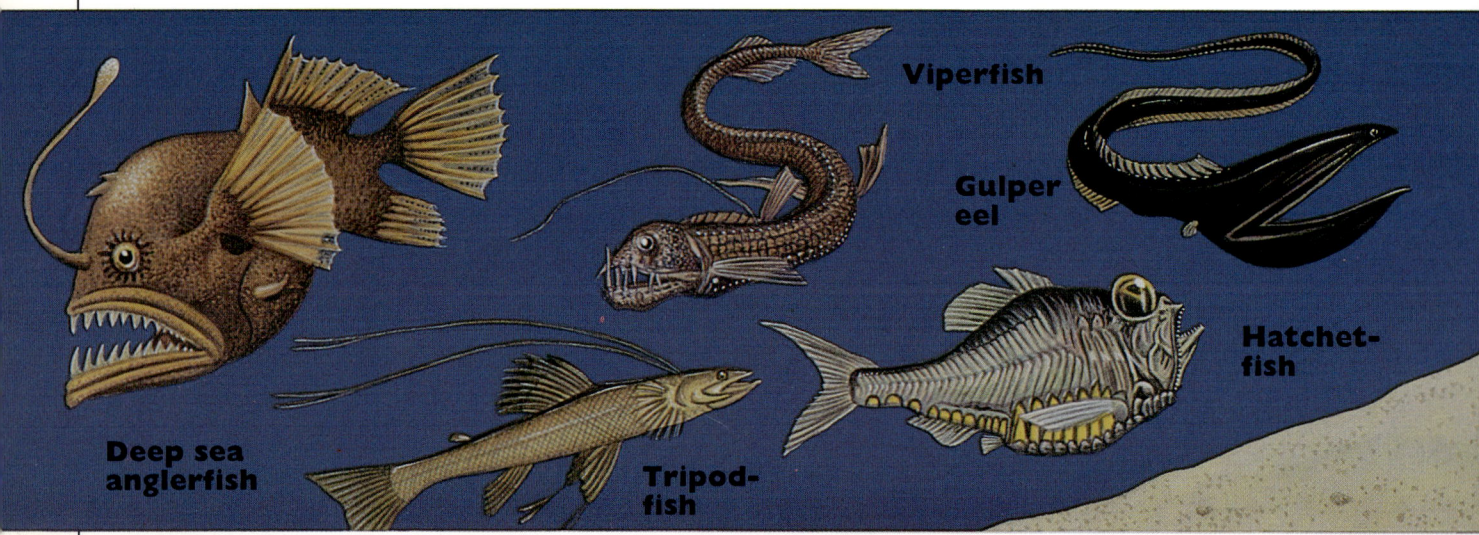

Viperfish

Gulper eel

Hatchet-fish

Deep sea anglerfish

Tripod-fish

Light-making fish

It is estimated that more than 1,000 species of fish produce light. Most live in the twilight zone of 100-500 metres depth. The production of light by living things is known as bioluminescence. In some fish, the glow is produced by chemical reactions in the skin, often involving the substance luciferase. In others the light comes from microscopic bacteria that live naturally in the fish's flesh. Luminous fish include flashlightfish, midshipmen, anglerfish, lanternfish and the dragonfish (shown right). The light may be to attract mates, illuminate prey or confuse predators.

Flattened fish

Many sea-bed fish are flattened in shape, and camouflaged to blend in with the gravel or weed. They can rest unnoticed on the sea bed, sometimes part-buried in the sand or gravel. One group is the rays (relatives of sharks, see page 17), which are flattened from top to bottom and lie on their undersides. Another group is the flatfishes such as plaice, sole and flounder. The largest flatfish species is the halibut, over two metres long, which is a deep-water predator of crabs, shellfish and fish. Plaice and turbot can vary their colouring to blend in with the bottom.

The travels of the eel

Adult eels leave the lakes and rivers of Europe and swim across the Atlantic to an area of warm water, the Sargasso Sea, where they breed. The babies drift back in ocean currents over four years. They change into see-through elvers, and head back up the rivers to grow into adults.

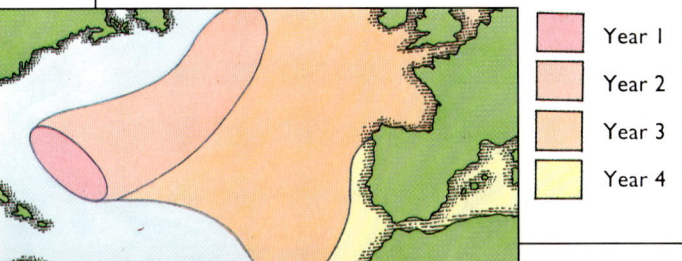

(pink)	Year 1
(light pink)	Year 2
(orange)	Year 3
(yellow)	Year 4

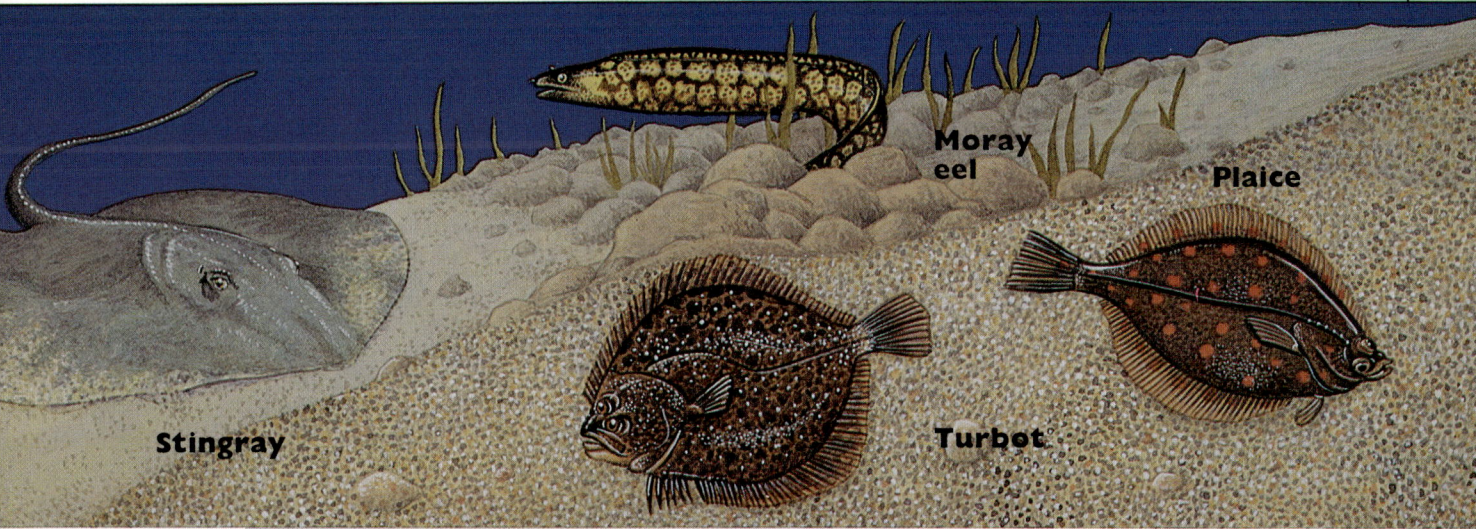

Stingray

Moray eel

Plaice

Turbot

Eyes right

A newly hatched flatfish such as the common sole is only three millimetres long and has the normal, upright fish shape. After about two weeks, at a length of five millimetres, one eye slowly begins to move around to the other side of the head.

By three weeks the body has become thinner, both eyes are on the one side, and the young flatfish starts to lean over and swim on its other, "blind" side. The sole, plaice and flounder usually lie left side down, while the turbot and brill lie on their right. However, individuals of the opposite orientation are found in all of these species.

Egg

10 days

2 weeks (from blind side)

3 weeks

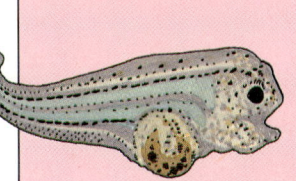

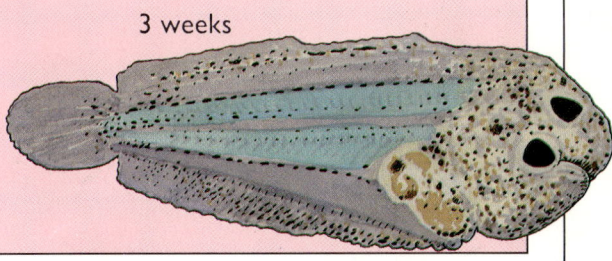

FISHING PAST & PRESENT

People have fished since prehistoric times. Fossil finds of stone-age humans such as Neanderthalers and Cro-Magnons show that these early people made fish hooks and harpoons over 30,000 years ago. Various traditional fishing methods have been described in this book. Many people also fish for leisure and sport; in Britain, for example, angling is the most popular participant sport. Today, however, the fishing industry faces a crisis. Commercial fishing is now so effective and widespread that some parts of the seas are fished out, and may never recover.

Fisher of men

In the early days of Christianity the first Christians were persecuted for their beliefs. In hiding they used the image of the fish as a secret symbol for Jesus Christ. The New Testament tells how Christ chose his twelve disciples, or closest followers, from the poor fishermen of the Sea of Galilee, so Christ himself became known as the "fisher of men". The mosaic below represents Christ as a large fish twined round an anchor, surrounded by small fish which represent his disciples.

Mosaic from a 4th century tomb in Tunisia, North Africa

Purse-seine net

A great invention

The humble fishfinger is one of the marketing successes of this century. For many years people had eaten fish "steaks" – large chunks of flesh. But this method of preparation gave many leftovers. So the excess bits were flaked and formed into rectangular slabs, in batter or breadcrumb containers. Fishfingers now account for over two-thirds of all fish consumed in Britain.

Fishing boats

Old-time fishing boats were crewed by sailors who were familiar with the traditional catching grounds, and knew how these varied with the weather and seasons. But chance played a large part in the results of their fishing trips. Today, chance has a much smaller part. The crews on modern vessels have the old knowledge, and also the help of high-tech machinery and scientific aids. They can preserve the fish they catch by placing them in freezers on board ship, and so stay at sea for longer periods – and catch more fish.

Farming fish

Fish are farmed in different ways around the world. Carp are reared in small ponds all over China. Elsewhere species such as salmon are farmed on a large scale, in fenced pens in estuaries, or metal cages floating in lakes and seas. In Japan, hundreds of artificial "reefs" have been built along the coastline, from waste concrete and building rubble. Fish and other marine life soon thrive in the sheltered waters, a method called inshore fish-rearing. In the United States, about one-tenth of the yearly fish harvest comes from farming, or aquaculture. This includes almost all of the rainbow trout and catfish caught there.

Nets and traps

The purse-seine net is trailed around the fish and then pulled tight like a gigantic draw-string purse. The trawl is a large net bag that is towed along the sea bed to trap species that swim near the bottom, such as cod and haddock. The gill net is like a huge curtain and traps fish by their gills. It is used for species that swim near the surface, such as herring and mackerel. Trolling involves towing hooks on lines often many kilometres long. Fish and shellfish are also caught in traps.

Trawl net

Gill net

Trolling

Trapping

The pleasures of fishing

English writer Izaak Walton produced his most famous book, *The Compleat Angler*, in 1653. It is a charming combination of poems, quotations and advice about fishing, descriptions of fish and their habits, true angling stories and fishy tales about "the ones that got away". It has been admired by anglers ever since.

Too easy to catch

While governments argue over catch quotas and regulations, the numbers of fish in the sea are declining. Sonar is a system like radar, but which uses sound waves underwater. The sound waves are beamed out from a transmitter and reflect off objects such as shoals of fish. The echoes are detected by a receiver, and the echo pattern is analysed by computer. As technological aids progress, fishing vessels can find their catches ever more easily, putting many species at risk.

CLASSIFICATION

Fish make up the large group called Pisces. This is one of the main groups of vertebrates, which also includes amphibians, reptiles, birds and mammals. Within the fish superclass, there are three main classes, as shown below. Fish classification has altered over the years, and there are still several different schemes. The bony fishes or teleosts are overwhelmingly the most numerous, both in terms of species, and of individuals in each species. The subgroup of bony fishes called the Percomorphids – perch-like fishes – make up almost half of all species of bony fishes.

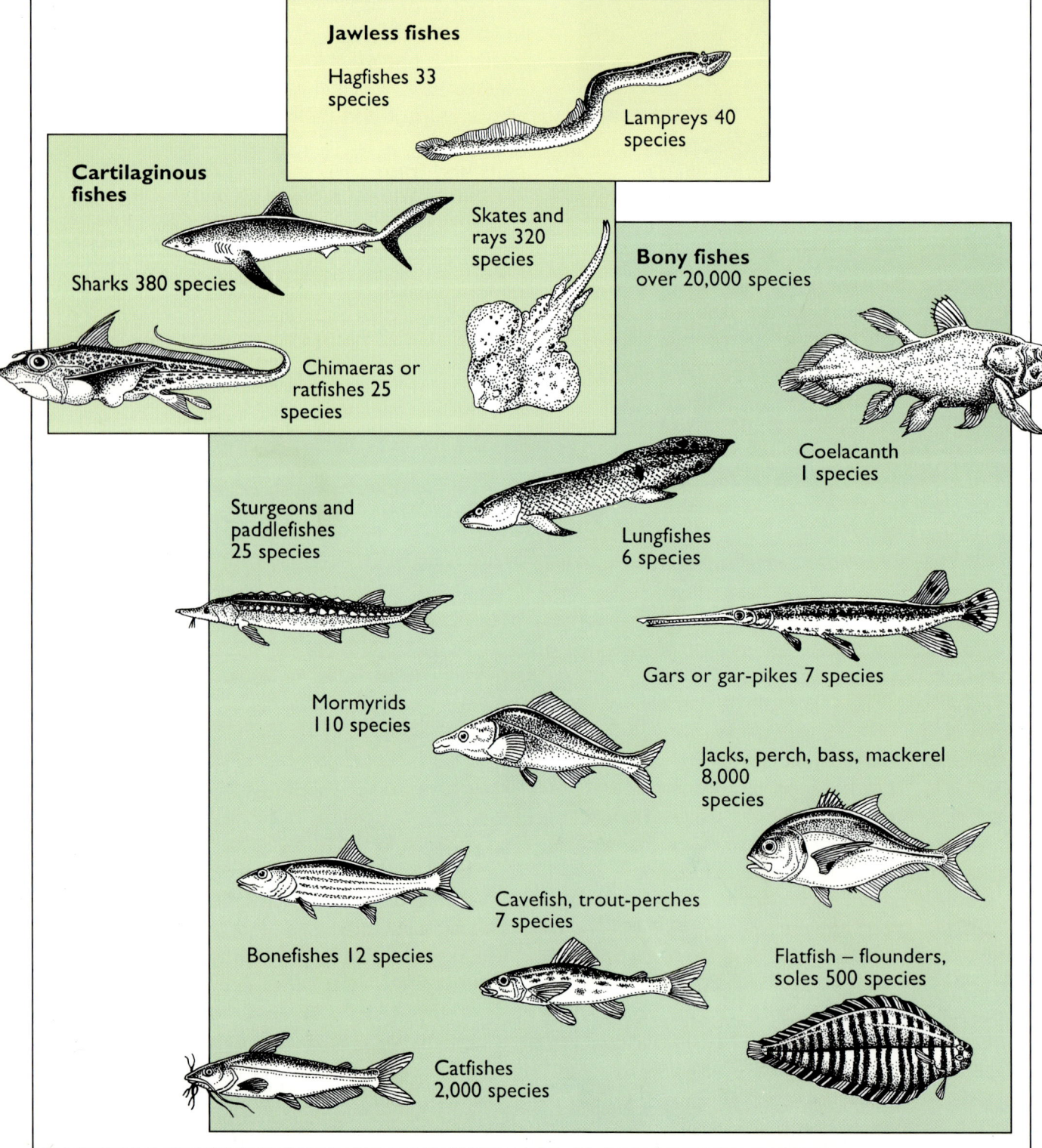

Jawless fishes

Hagfishes 33 species

Lampreys 40 species

Cartilaginous fishes

Sharks 380 species

Skates and rays 320 species

Chimaeras or ratfishes 25 species

Bony fishes over 20,000 species

Coelacanth 1 species

Sturgeons and paddlefishes 25 species

Lungfishes 6 species

Gars or gar-pikes 7 species

Mormyrids 110 species

Jacks, perch, bass, mackerel 8,000 species

Bonefishes 12 species

Cavefish, trout-perches 7 species

Flatfish – flounders, soles 500 species

Catfishes 2,000 species

GLOSSARY

Barbels Slim, fleshy tentacles or "whiskers" around the lower mouth of many fish. They are especially well developed in fish such as catfish, the barbel itself, and deep-sea species like the anglerfish. Barbels are very sensitive, detecting touch and chemicals in the water.

Bioluminescence The production of light by living things. Hundreds of kinds of fish are bioluminescent, especially in the dark deep sea.

Camouflage Patterns and colours on an animal's body which make it blend in with the background, so it is difficult to see.

Chemosenses Animal senses that detect chemicals. In humans, they are smell and taste, which are separate. In a fish, both smell and taste detect chemicals floating in the water. So the distinction between smell and taste is less clear.

Denticles Tiny, tooth-shaped scales in the skin of a shark. Much larger, stronger denticles form the shark's teeth.

Electrosensors Tiny pits or bumps on a fish's skin that are sensitive to electricity in the water. Many fish have electrosensors, from sharks to electric eels and elephant-snout fish. They are usually on or around the head end.

Fin A broad, flat surface projecting from the fish's body, used for swimming and manoeuvring in the water. Fins on certain parts of the body have their own name, for example, the one at the rear end is the caudal fin (tail). Some specialised fins are shaped like spines or muscular limbs.

Gills The "breathing" parts of a fish, which do the same job as the lungs of a land animal. Gills are designed to extract oxygen dissolved in the water. They are usually feathery, blood-rich parts behind the head.

Lateral line A thin strip along each side of a fish's body, which usually shows up as a shiny or light-coloured line. It senses water currents, helping the fish to feel its way.

Milt Fish sperm, released by the male.

Parasite A plant or animal which eats or feeds on another plant or animal, called the host, while it is still alive. Some male fish, like the deep-sea angler, attach to the female and live as a parasite on her. The lampreys are parasitic on larger fish.

Pharyngeal teeth Teeth in the back of the mouth, around the throat region. They are very well developed in some fish, such as flatfishes. They are usually broad and flat, and used for crushing and grinding.

Predator A hunting animal, that catches and eats other animals, called prey.

Prey An animal that becomes the victim of a predator, and is caught and eaten.

Roe Fish eggs, laid by the female.

Shoal A group of fish, which usually stay close to each other and swim together in a coordinated way. Another name for a shoal is a school.

Spawning The time period when fish breed, and also the name of the breeding process itself. The female lays her eggs and the male fertilises them with his sperm.

Symbiosis A partnership or relationship between two different types of living things, such as a sea anemone and a fish, where both partners benefit.

Swim bladder A gas-filled chamber inside the fish's body, that works as an adjustable float. Its size can be altered to change the fish's buoyancy, so the fish can float at different depths, and dive or rise.

INDEX

Photocredits

ABBREVIATIONS: T-top, M-middle, B-bottom,
L-left, R-right
Front cover, 3b, 6, 7t, 8, 11b, 20, 22t, 24,28t
& b: Roger Vlitos; 2t,3t,4,5 both, 7bl, 8-9,
10,11t & m, 12-13 all, 14,15t, 18 all, 23
both, 26t, 28-29 & 29t: Bruce Coleman Ltd;
2b, 16: Universal (Courtesy Kobal Collection);
7br, 15b, 19b, 22br, 26b, 28m: Planet Earth
Pictures; 9b, 19t, 22bl, 29b: Mary Evans
Picture Library